Preschool Skills

Beginning Sounds

Illustrations by **Nathan Jarvis**

An imprint of Sterling Children's Books

Published by Sterling Publishing Co., Inc.
387 Park Avenue South, New York, NY 10016
Text and illustrations © 2005 by Flash Kids
Distributed in Canada by Sterling Publishing
c/o Canadian Manda Group, 165 Dufferin Street
Toronto, Ontario, Canada M6K 3H6
Distributed in the United Kingdom by GMC Distribution Services
Castle Place, 166 High Street, Lewes, East Sussex, England BN7 1XU
Distributed in Australia by Capricorn Link (Australia) Pty. Ltd.
P.O. Box 704, Windsor, NSW 2756, Australia

Sterling ISBN 978-1-4114-3422-6

Manufactured in Canada

Lot #:
12 14 16 15 13
03/14

For information about custom editions, special sales, premium and
corporate purchases, please contact Sterling Special Sales
Department at 800-805-5489 or specialsales@sterlingpublishing.com.

Cover illustrations, design, and production by Mada Design, Inc.

Dear Parent,

Help your child build a solid foundation for reading and writing with this Preschool Skills workbook. Colorful illustrations and fun activities introduce basic beginning letter sounds. Help your child make the most of this workbook with these tips:

- Provide a quiet, comfortable place for your child to complete this workbook. Go through each page with him or her slowly to ensure full comprehension of each activity.

- If your child answers a question incorrectly, explain why it is incorrect and allow your child to correct the mistake.

- Encourage your child to ask questions and have discussions about the things your child finds interesting in this book. You can also ask your child questions to keep him or her engaged in learning.

- Try to relate concepts found in this book to things your child encounters in everyday life. For example, have your child identify letter sounds in familiar words—household objects, family members' names, and street signs.

- Most of all, enjoy this special time spent together! Reading to your child and helping him or her learn will build a strong bond between you both.

Dancing Ducks

Duck begins with the **D** sound.
Circle all the things in the picture
that **begin** with the **D** sound.

Circle the thing in each row that **begins** with the **same** sound as the first one.

harmonica	hammer	nail	saw
piano	apple	banana	pineapple
drum	cat	dog	mouse
guitar	flower	tree	grass

Draw a line to match the things that **begin** with the **same** sound.

fox

dog

ostrich

hippo

duck

fish

hamster

octopus

Goat in the Grass

Goat begins with the **G** sound.
Circle all the things in the picture
that **begin** with the **G** sound.

Gwen's Garden

Monkey begins with the **M** sound.
Help the monkey find its mother.

What letter did you make?

Cross out the things that **do not begin** with the **P** sound.

penguin

cookie

pencil

book

pear

peach

Circle the thing in each row that **begins** with the **same** sound as the first one.

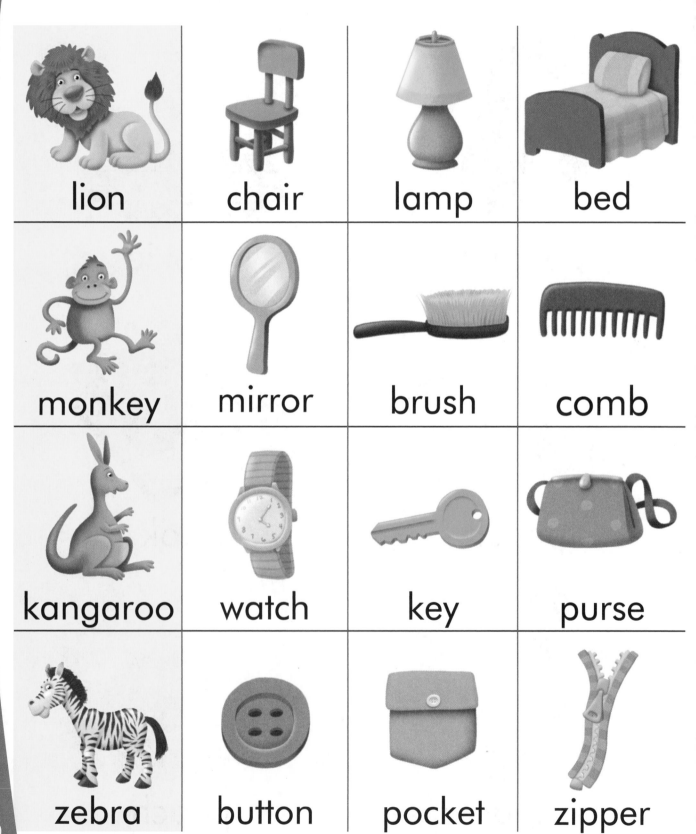

lion	chair	lamp	bed
monkey	mirror	brush	comb
kangaroo	watch	key	purse
zebra	button	pocket	zipper

Kicky Kangaroo

Kangaroo begins with the **K** sound. Circle all the things in the picture that **begin** with the **K** sound.

Draw a line to match the things that **begin** with the **same** sound.

boat

dominos

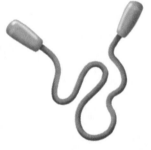

jump rope

truck

top

jacks

doll

bear

Circle the thing in each row that **begins** with the **same** sound as the first one.

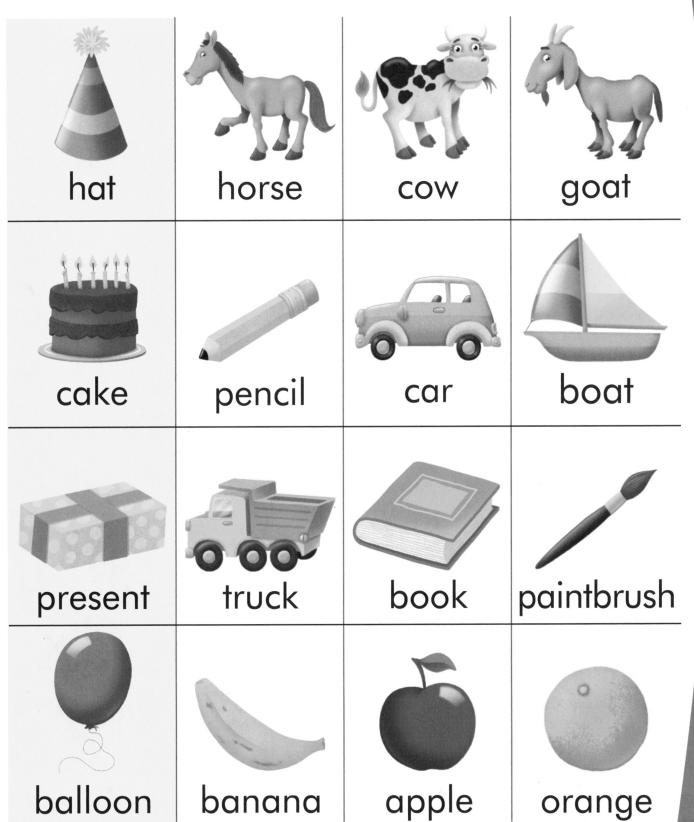

hat	horse	cow	goat
cake	pencil	car	boat
present	truck	book	paintbrush
balloon	banana	apple	orange

13

Snake begins with the **S** sound.
Help the snake find the sun and sand.

What letter did you make?

Running in the Rain

Run begins with the **R** sound.
Circle all the things in the picture
that **begin** with the **R** sound.

Quiet begins with the **Q** sound. Cross out the things that **do not begin** with the **Q** sound.

queen

ring

quilt

duck

quarter

Draw a line to match the things that **begin** with the **same** sound.

cake

peach

bread

juice

pie

cookie

jelly

banana

Lion begins with the **L** sound.
Help the lion find its lunch.

What letter did you make?

Circle the thing in each row that **begins** with the **same** sound as the first one.

ball	chicken	mop	broom
glove	goat	bat	horse
cap	lettuce	carrot	pumpkin
shoe	shell	rock	flower

19

Nest begins with the **N** sound.
Cross out the things that **do not begin** with the **N** sound.

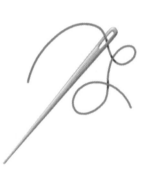

needle

vest

noodles

nut

monkey

nose

In an Igloo

Igloo begins with the **I** sound. Circle all the things in the picture that **begin** with the **I** sound.

Umbrella begins with the **U** sound.
Help Uncle Umberto find his umbrella.

What letter did you make?

Circle the thing in each row that **begins** with the **same** sound as the first one.

plate	tree	sun	plant
cup	elephant	clown	balloon
fork	rabbit	fox	skunk
spoon	spatula	bowl	pan

23

Alligator begins with the **A** sound. Cross out the things that **do not begin** with the **A** sound.

ant

apple

car

airplane

dog

ax

Draw a line to match the things that **begin** with the **same** sound.

ball

glove

helmet

shoe

skate

bat

goal

hoop

Walrus begins with the **W** sound.
Help Walter Walrus find
his friend Wendy Whale.

What letter did you make?

Circle the thing in each row that **begins** with the **same** sound as the first one.

bag	lion	tiger	bear
apple	ant	butterfly	snail
milk	man	baby	girl
sandwich	flower	tree	sun

Time for T

Time begins with the **T** sound. Circle all the things in the picture that **begin** with the **T** sound.

Elbow begins with the **E** sound. Cross out the things that **do not begin** with the **E** sound.

egg

bread

elephant

elf

cow

eagle

Draw a line to match the things that **begin** with the **same** sound.

clown

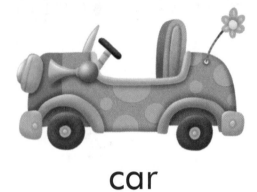

car

tiger

juggle

popcorn

tent

jump

peanuts

Violin begins with the **V** sound.
Help Victor find his violin.

What letter did you make?

Circle the thing in each row that **begins** with the **same** sound as the first one.

soap	butterfly	snail	ladybug
towel	turtle	frog	snake
duck	seal	dolphin	crab
robe	bird	cloud	rainbow

Yesterday begins with the **Y** sound.
Cross out the things that
do not begin with the **Y** sound.

yellow

fox

yarn

yak

doll

yo-yo

A Quiet Queen

Quiet begins with the **Q** sound. Circle all the things in the picture that **begin** with the **Q** sound.

Draw a line to match the things that **begin** with the **same** sound.

baby

doll

crib

cry

diaper

bottle

horse

hat

Circle the thing in each row that **begins** with the **same** sound as the first one.

wheelbarrow	hat	watch	belt
tomato	table	chair	rug
lettuce	grass	flower	leaf
rabbit	dress	ring	vest

Zebra begins with the **Z** sound.
Help the zebra find its way to the zoo.

What letter did you make?

Ostrich begins with the **O** sound. Cross out the things that **do not begin** with the **O** sound.

orange

otter

nest

octopus

tree

olive

A Fine Day

Fine begins with the **F** sound.
Circle all the things in the picture
that **begin** with the **F** sound.

Draw a line to match the things that **begin** with the **same** sound.

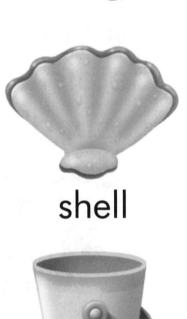

shell

ball

bucket

family

hat

sand

fish

hot

Circle the thing in each row that **begins** with the **same** sound as the first one.

toothbrush	lettuce	tomato	carrot
pillow	crayon	book	pencil
blanket	ball	glove	cap
moon	lion	monkey	tiger

41

Cat begins with the **C** sound.
Help the cat find the comfy couch.

What letter did you make?

Violet begins with the **V** sound.
Cross out the things that
do not begin with the **V** sound.

vest

bee

violin

valentine

broom

vacuum

43

What a Mess!

Mess begins with the **M** sound.
Circle all the things in the picture
that **begin** with the **M** sound.

Circle the thing in each row that **begins** with the **same** sound as the first one.

turtle	sun	flower	tree
frog	eye	hand	foot
snake	butterfly	snail	ladybug
lizard	lamp	chair	table

Say the name of each picture.
Write the **beginning** sound.

apple a

boat b

cat c

doll d

egg e

fish f

Say the name of each picture. Write the **beginning** sound.

goat   g

hat   h

igloo   i

jar   j

key   k

lamp   l

47

Say the name of each picture. Write the **beginning** sound.

moon __ m

nest __ n

octopus __ o

pencil __ p

quarter __ q   rake __ r   sun __ s

Say the name of each picture.
Write the **beginning** sound.

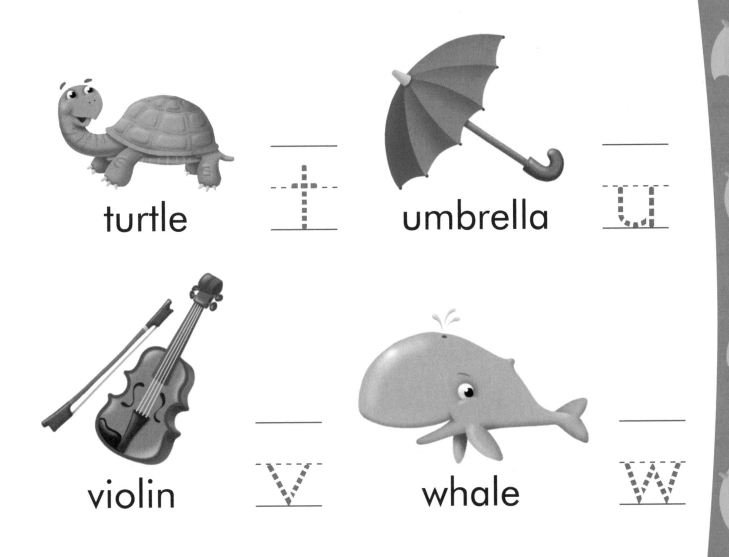

turtle ___t___

umbrella ___U___

violin ___V___

whale ___W___

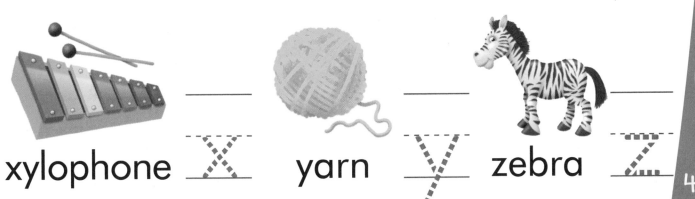

xylophone ___X___   yarn ___Y___   zebra ___Z___

Draw a line from each picture to its **beginning** sound.

N

I

E

L

Draw a line from each picture to its **beginning** sound.

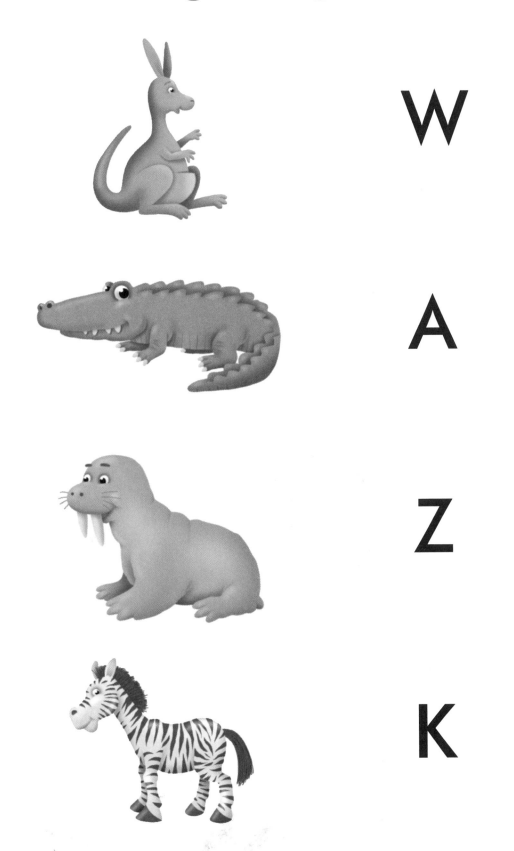

W

A

Z

K

Draw a line from each picture to its **beginning** sound.

X

P

G

V

Draw a line from each picture to its **beginning** sound.

A

B

S

O

Cross out the thing in each row that **does not begin** with the letter sound shown.

H

I

K

O

Cross out the thing in each row that **does not begin** with the letter sound shown.

Q

U

Y

R

Cross out the thing in each row that **does not begin** with the letter sound shown.

T

F

D

C

Cross out the thing in each row that **does not begin** with the letter sound shown.

J

M

L

N

  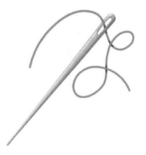

Circle the letter that makes the **beginning** sound for each picture.

boat

a   b   c

train

r   s   t

car

c   d   e

airplane

a   b   c

Circle the letter that makes the **beginning** sound for each picture.

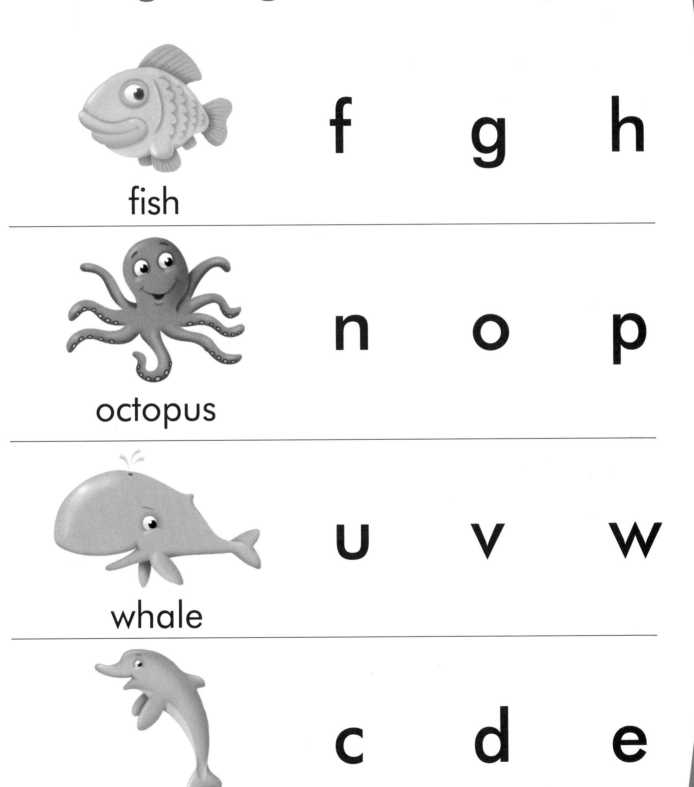

fish

f   g   h

octopus

n   o   p

whale

U   v   W

dolphin

c   d   e

Circle the letter that makes the **beginning** sound for each picture.

tree

r   s   t

nest

n   o   p

bird

b   c   d

worm

v   w   x

Circle the letter that makes the **beginning** sound for each picture.

shoes   s   t   u

hat   g   h   i

jacket   h   i   j

pants   o   p   q

Circle the letter that makes the **beginning** sound for each picture.

cow

a   b   c

goat

f   g   h

duck

d   e   f

mouse

l   m   n

Circle the letter that makes the **beginning** sound for each picture.

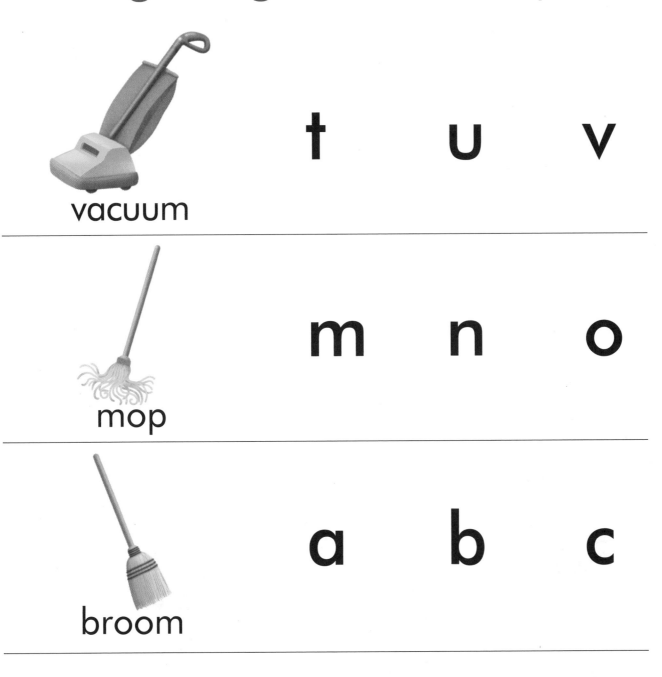

vacuum

t   u   v

mop

m   n   o

broom

a   b   c

sponge

s   t   u

Good work,

_____ !
(Name)

You are ready to read!